Classic children's books are a perfect addition to any language arts program. These timeless stories have brought pleasure and inspiration to generations of young readers. This series makes these revered works accessible to students and will encourage them to read the books in their original versions. Encouraging children to read great literature opens new worlds of adventure, language, travel, history, suspense, and mystery.

———————————

Oliver Twist by Charles Dickens is a heart-wrenching novel about a poor boy and his journey from the workhouse of nineteenth-century England to the discovery of his true origins. Throughout the book, the author instructs the reader on the realities of English life at the time in which he and Oliver lived. It is an excellent example of how someone may triumph in the face of great adversity if that person possesses a sense of self, basic decency, and determination.

———————————

Here are some suggestions for introducing *Oliver Twist* to students:

- Ask students how they would react if an orphan in trouble appeared at their door.

- As students read the story, ask them to discuss any characters with traits they may have seen in people they've met.

Teaching the classics enriches students' education by

- exposing students to a wide variety of genres

- introducing students to great literature

- helping students to become familiar with how people lived in other times and places

- encouraging students to relate the experiences of others to themselves

- providing opportunities for increased vocabulary development

- increasing awareness of society's values

- encouraging independent thinking as students explore an author's point of view

CHARLES DICKENS

Charles Dickens wrote many books filled with lively and colorful characters. When he was young, changes were occurring in England. Slavery was abolished and laws were established to protect children who worked. But England had a growing population of the poor. The Poor Law of 1834 sentenced paupers, those with no money and no means of support, to the workhouse. This included young children. In the workhouse, young and old were worked hard and were fed little. Many died. People who lived in the workhouses were looked down upon by those who didn't. Although these institutions were very harsh, they had, within three years, greatly reduced the cost of caring for the poor. But this harshness also produced more criminals than ever. The workhouse, and the terrible life within its walls, was Dickens's target when he wrote *Oliver Twist*. The fictional Oliver was much luckier than most real orphans. Dickens was obviously touched by the lives of poor children and certainly made the public aware of their circumstances.

Dickens was born in 1812. Although his father had a job, he spent more money than he earned and was eventually thrown in debtors' prison, along with his wife and four of their children. Charles escaped the prison life because he had a job in a warehouse. During this time, the impressionable and sensitive boy lived with ruffians and had little to eat. He had, however, a great determination to succeed. At the time of his death in 1870, he was beloved by readers on both sides of the Atlantic and the whole world mourned his passing.

Oliver Twist

Oliver Twist is set in nineteenth-century England during the Industrial Revolution. This book tells the story of a child born in poverty and destined for the workhouse, the notorious place where paupers were sent to work and be starved until they either died, obtained gainful employment, or turned to lives of crime. Oliver seems to be a boy with no family and no luck, but he finds both after enduring much hardship and sorrow. Oliver's story is fiction, but it mirrors the plight of many youngsters during this time.

FS-17020 Oliver Twist (retold)

A London Museum

Create a museum of objects from and books about London. Have students display the items as they would find them displayed in a museum. (Coins and stamps can be arranged on a piece of dark cloth so they can be plainly seen. A small card that identifies and tells about each item should be placed next to each display.) Consider displaying the following items:

- maps, travel posters, and postcards that show London
- coins and stamps from England
- pictures of Queen Victoria, Dickens, and famous people of the 1800s
- books by Dickens and his contemporaries

Come and See Our Exhibit!

Have students make posters advertising their London "museum exhibition." Show students examples of posters that museums create to tell the public about their new exhibits. Then let groups of students create posters that invite their schoolmates to tour their museum. Have students draw pictures that illustrate items that can be seen at their classroom museum on large pieces of posterboard. Tell students to include on the poster an invitation to come and see the exhibit, what time the exhibit is available for viewing, and how many days the exhibit will be displayed. Then help students to put up their posters in appropriate places on the school grounds. During "museum hours," student volunteers can conduct tours of the exhibit and tell information they have learned about the items on display to interested schoolmates.

Where in the World?

Have groups of students research places that are mentioned in the story. Provide them with maps of England and London and encyclopedias so they can find out more about the world of Oliver Twist. Assign the following places:

- London
- the workhouse
- Chertsey, Pentonville, and other London suburbs

To give students an added understanding of the class differences in nineteenth century London, split each of the place categories between two or more groups and have each group research what life was like in that place for members of a particular class. (Example: London for the wealthy, for the middle-class tradesman, and for the poor) Ask a student volunteer from each group to present its findings to the class.

Introducing the Story

Tell your students about the great movement toward social reform that began in England in the first part of the nineteenth century. Explain to your students that at that time there was great inequity in how the rich and the poor were treated and represented by their government. Many of the progressive thinkers of that time believed that this inequity was not only wrong but that they could change it. Many writers, Dickens included, felt that the purpose of the novel was to inform the public of the need for social reform. With *Oliver Twist*, Dickens exposes what the harsh life of the workhouse does to the good people that find themselves trapped in a life that can only lead to crime and despair. Dickens uses the people and events in the life of young Oliver to show the impact of evil influences on impressionable young boys. Fagin and the boys who took Oliver in were the nineteenth-century equivalent of a modern street gang. Ask students to think about the choices Oliver had to make and the choices that they and their friends have had to make. Ask them to discuss any similarities and differences they notice.

Some of these words are old-fashioned but necessary to retain the flavor of the story. Have students look up and write sentences with the vocabulary words to enhance their reading experience.

CHAPTER 1
orphan
workhouse
beadle
oakum
gruel
cast lots
apprentice

CHAPTER 2
chimney sweep
magistrate
undertaker

CHAPTER 3
repulsive
distinguished
tenements
pummeled
wretched
slander
box
insolence
ranting
raving

CHAPTER 4
departure
observed
feebly
perished

CHAPTER 5
disreputable
curious
stout
hearty

CHAPTER 6
perpetrator

harshly
criminals
bellowed
disgustedly
bookstall
prophecy
colossal
pavement
coach

CHAPTER 7
verge
demise
portrait
scurried
residence

CHAPTER 8
consciousness
mealy
remarkable
cautioned

CHAPTER 9
drat
paupers
stubborn
soothed
absconded
enticed
treachery
ingratitude
malice
foundling
earnest

CHAPTER 10
constantly
betray
regaled

despicable
stupor

CHAPTER 11
heed
infamous
gruesome
transported
hubbub
unsavory
squalid
lollygag
sorely
pantry

CHAPTER 12
matron
utterance

CHAPTER 13
dogging
throttled

CHAPTER 14
survey
rummage
unearthed
flustered
vexing
lolling

CHAPTER 15
posse
pursuit
bungled
intruders
engrossed
sordid

CHAPTER 16
gratitude
obviously
balmy
tutor

CHAPTER 17
collided
suitable
reconsider
whereabouts

CHAPTER 18
fishwife
tavern
cloak
pawnbroker

CHAPTER 19
tended
waylaid
villains

CHAPTER 20
lagging
mockery
dastardly

CHAPTER 21
short-lived
enraged

CHAPTER 22
fraud
ultimately
defiantly
restitution
noose

CHAPTER 1

ORPHANED

The young woman in the bed looked very sick indeed. She had just given birth to a baby boy, but she would not live to see him grow up.

"Let me see the child and die," she whispered to the doctor and old woman who were in attendance at the birth. The old woman handed the young mother her baby.

"Another orphan brat!" the doctor complained. "How came the mother here to the workhouse?"

The woman shook her head. "She was found in the street, practically dead. She'd no doubt been on the streets for a while, as her shoes were all worn out."

"No mother, no father. He'll be sent to the workhouse. No matter," declared the doctor, who had seen it all many times before.

The young woman held her baby, then died. No one knew her name or that of her family. She seemed to be just another poor woman, worth nothing.

They wrapped the baby in dirty linen that had been used for many before him. He was farmed out to Mrs. Mann, who maintained these scrawny orphans with a fraction of the money she was given for them. Most of the money went into her own pocket.

Miraculously, the boy survived. He remained with Mrs. Mann and other children like himself. And one day, when he was nine years old, Mr. Bumble, the local beadle, came to call.

Mrs. Mann looked forward to Mr. Bumble's visits.

"Mr. Bumble, how did the boy come to be named Oliver Twist?" she asked with some curiosity.

Mr. Bumble answered with a touch of pride, "I named him! You see, the one before him was named Swubble, and T comes after S, so I named him Twist. I have names ready for each one of them in turn. No one ever did discover who or where he came from. Now he's nine, and too old to remain in your gentle care, kind lady." Mrs. Mann blushed at the compliment. "I will take him now, as he's old enough to go to the workhouse." Oliver was called and appeared before the beadle. He had

FS-17020 Oliver Twist (retold)

many layers of dirt on his person, and he was thin and pale.

"Would you like to come with me?" Mr. Bumble asked. Oliver shook his head yes. What could be worse than starving every day under the eye of Mrs. Mann?

Soon after he arrived at the workhouse, Oliver was summoned by the board, a group of eight or ten fat gentlemen who ran the workhouse and made decisions affecting it. The boy burst into tears.

"Do you know you're an orphan?" one of the board members asked.

"What's that, sir?" Oliver asked tearfully.

"Hmph! The boy's a fool!" suggested another. "You must be educated and learn a trade," he declared. "Tomorrow you will begin to pick oakum!" Oliver was led away to a room filled with beds. He fell asleep, crying, on a bed hard as rocks.

The first six months in the workhouse were the hardest Oliver had ever known, even in his short, miserable life. He worked all day and was fed a bit of watery gruel and occasionally some bread for his meager meals. He and the other boys were on the brink of starvation. Finally, they could tolerate their hunger no longer. The boys cast lots to see who would ask for more food. As luck would have it, it fell upon Oliver.

Oliver nervously walked toward the master of the workhouse with his bowl and spoon in hand. "Please, sir, I want some more," he spoke. The master, who was very well fed himself, glared at the child.

"What?" he asked in a faint voice. Oliver repeated, "Please, sir, I want some more." The master hit Oliver in the head with a ladle, then ran to tell the board. "He asked for more!" the master trembled as he said it. The board agreed that Oliver was no good, ungrateful, and destined to be hanged some day.

Oliver was punished by being locked in a dark, small room. At mealtimes he was taken before the boys and beaten as an example to those who would also show ingratitude for the proper life they were granted. The board decided it was time to offer the young beggar as an apprentice to anyone who would take him for a small fee.

FS-17020 Oliver Twist (retold)

Name _____

1. While living with Mrs. Mann, Oliver was dirty, thin, and pale. Draw a picture of what you think Oliver would have looked like if he had parents and a home of his own.

2. Why do you think Mrs. Mann, Mr. Bumble, and the board were so cruel to the orphans?

_____

_____

3. What do you think should have happened to Oliver after his mother died? _____

_____

_____

4. Do you think children Oliver's age should be working? Why or why not? _____

_____

_____

5. What would you have done in Oliver's place to make things better? Would he have been able to do so? _____

_____

_____

© Frank Schaffer Publications, Inc.   FS-17020 Oliver Twist (retold)

CHAPTER 2

GOOD-BYE TO THE WORKHOUSE

One day, a particularly disgusting man, Mr. Ganfield, appeared at the workhouse to take advantage of the offer. He would be given five pounds to take Oliver off their hands. Mr. Limbkins of the board asked Mr. Ganfield what his business was. "I'm a chimney sweep," he said, beady eyes gleaming. "The best there is. It's a fitting trade for a young lad."

Mr. Limbkins countered, "It's a nasty trade." But he later decided to give Oliver to Mr. Ganfield if he would agree to a little less money. The chimney sweep agreed and the papers were drawn up. Oliver would become a chimney sweep. The trembling boy was brought before the magistrates.

"Please, sirs," pleaded Oliver, "don't send me with that gentleman. I'd take anything else." The boy's terror didn't go unnoticed.

"Very well," agreed a kindly old magistrate. "You may return, for now, to the workhouse."

The sign advertising Oliver's availability was again posted. And so it was that the undertaker, Mr. Sowerberry, agreed to take the boy on a trial basis to see if he would work out.

Oliver didn't move a muscle when told about his fate. "He's a hardened rascal," stated one of the board.

Oliver was taken to the undertaker's. On the way, he cried terribly. Mr. Bumble ordered him to stop. "Oh, sir," cried Oliver, "I'm so alone. Everybody hates me." Mr. Bumble didn't know what to make of this outburst.

At the undertaker's, Mrs. Sowerberry, the undertaker's wife, approached the boy.

"Here, you," she said, "You can have whatever the dog leaves behind. When you're done, you'll sleep in that space underneath the counters, next to the coffins. You shouldn't mind that."

Fortunately for Oliver, the dog had left some tasty pieces of food. The hungry boy tore into them and gobbled them up, to the astonishment of Mrs. Sowerberry. She led him to his bed.

FS-17020 Oliver Twist (retold)

Name _____

1. What do you think a chimney sweep does? Why did Mr. Limbkins call it "a nasty trade"? _____
   _____

2. Why didn't Oliver want to go with the chimney sweep? _____
   _____

3. If you were going to be apprenticed to someone, what job would you choose? Why? _____
   _____

4. Why do you think Mr. Bumble didn't answer Oliver when the boy confided his feelings of
   loneliness to him? _____
   _____

5. Do you think the board truly felt they were treating the boys in their care fairly? Why or why not?
   _____

6. Why did Oliver gobble up the dog's leavings so eagerly? _____
   _____

7. If you were Oliver, what would you think of your life? _____
   _____

FS-17020 Oliver Twist (retold)

CHAPTER 3

THE APPRENTICE

When Oliver awoke, it was to a great clatter at the door. He had not slept happily and was frightened at what might await him in his new "home." Although he didn't know what was on the other side of the door, Oliver opened it. There stood a repulsive young man named Noah Claypole, distinguished by a large head and tiny eyes.

"Hey!" Noah exclaimed, "Get up and help me! You're the last one here. I came before you, so I'm the boss, and you better get used to doing what I tell you to do!" He administered a good, hard kick to Oliver and continued, "And, by the way, you'll call me Mr. Claypole!" Oliver was so frightened by the looks of this boy that he didn't dare protest. "Come on, help me take down the shutters," ordered the boy. "You look weak, but you better do your part or you'll get a good beating!"

Oliver was, in fact, left to take down the shutters alone. While taking them down he accidentally broke a pane of glass. For this he got a "good" beating.

Oliver had been with the Sowerberrys for a time when Mr. Sowerberry told him to go with him to pick up a body. They made their way through the worst tenements imaginable, until they arrived at a door. A man, shriveled and pale, let them in. An old woman, her face as wrinkled as an elephant's hide, was there, mourning the death of her daughter. The man was the dead woman's husband, and he was beside himself with grief.

"Keep away! You won't take my wife!" exclaimed the man. "They starved her to death! When will she be buried?" His children, now motherless, looked like skin and bones.

"We'll take her tomorrow," said the undertaker.

The next day Oliver and Mr. Sowerberry returned. They took the body in the coffin to the churchyard, where the gravediggers buried the poor woman. Mr. Sowerberry asked Oliver, "Well, boy, how do you like it?" Oliver hesitated, then admitted, "Not very much, sir."

"Well, never mind," replied the undertaker. "You'll get used to it."

After a month, Oliver's trial was up, and he became a regular apprentice to the undertaker. Business was good, and Oliver was kept very busy. Any small bit of appreciation for Oliver's work by Mr. Sowerberry just enraged Noah Claypole. Oliver was often beaten within an inch of his life by the jealous bully. But nothing Noah did to Oliver could make him angry enough to take on the older boy. Finally, however, Noah Claypole made Oliver angry.

"Where's your mother?" he asked. Oliver replied, "She's dead."

"I heard she died in the workhouse and she was a real bad one!" Noah taunted Oliver.

FS-17020 Oliver Twist (retold)

"Don't talk about my mother like that!" yelled Oliver. His spirit was alive again as he lunged at Noah and knocked the boy down.

"Help! Help!" yelled Noah. "He's going to kill me!"

Mrs. Sowerberry and Charlotte, a young servant, began to beat on Oliver and hold him down while Noah pummeled him from the back.

"Shall I call the police?" asked an eager Noah.

"No!" panted Mrs. Sowerberry, exhausted from the beating she was administering to Oliver. "Call Mr. Bumble! He'll know what to do!"

Noah ran for Mr. Bumble. When he found him, Noah yelled out such a tale of terror that Oliver had inflicted upon everyone that the beadle ran right to the undertaker's to give the orphan the flogging he deserved. After all, hadn't Noah, that poor, terrified young man, sworn that Oliver had tried to murder them all?

"You've been too good to this wretched boy!" exclaimed the beadle. "He's been eating meat! You should have kept him on gruel! He's from a bad family, you know!"

Oliver, hearing new slander against his mother, became violent. Just then Mr. Sowerberry returned and promptly gave Oliver a good box on the ear. "He called my mother names," said Oliver defiantly.

"Well, so what if he did?" replied the undertaker. "She deserved what he said, and worse!"

"She did not!" insisted the boy. "That's a lie!" For this insolence he was shut up and fed a little bread. Then he was allowed to go to his pitiful bed. From there, he could hear the ranting and raving continuing in the house, and there were quite a few remarks made about his unfortunate mother. Oliver noticed that he was not locked in, but could unfasten the door. He made his plans. He knew now what he had to do, but decided to wait for the first rays of light.

FS-17020 Oliver Twist (retold)

Name _____

1. What do you think of Noah's character? Describe what kind of person he was. _____
   _____
   _____

2. Why did Mr. Bumble think eating meat encouraged Oliver to misbehave? _____
   _____
   _____

3. Although he was beaten, do you think Oliver reacted correctly to the insults about his mother?
   Why or why not? _____
   _____
   _____

4. Think about what happened at the Sowerberry house. Draw a picture showing how you think the
   beadle, Charlotte, Mr. and Mrs. Sowerberry, and Noah looked after Oliver received his beating.

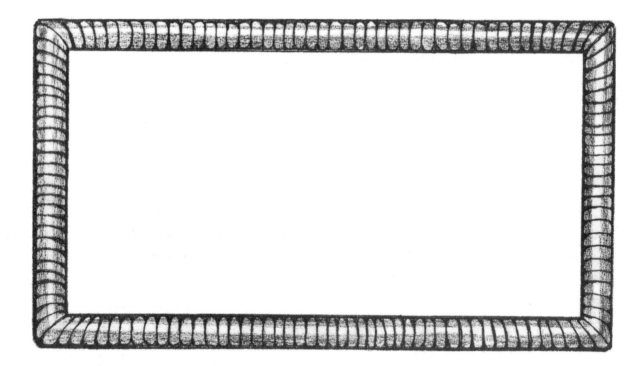

5. Why do you think Noah hated Oliver so much? _____
   _____
   _____
   _____

FS-17020 Oliver Twist (retold)

CHAPTER 4

THE RUNAWAY

As dawn broke, Oliver silently unbarred the door and crept out into the fresh air. He looked all about him, frightened that his departure might be observed. It was not, as far as he could determine.

Oliver walked the same path he'd walked when Mr. Bumble had taken him from Mrs. Mann's farm to the workhouse. As he neared the infant farm, he passed through a small garden. A thin, frail child was weeding it.

"Dick!" Oliver called softly. "Dick! It's me, Oliver! How are you, Dick?"

The boy looked delighted to see his old friend, as delighted as his tired, pale face could muster. The two boys had been beaten and starved together many, many times.

"I heard them say that I'm dying," the boy replied softly. "I know it's true, because I dream of heaven and angels and kind words I never hear when I'm awake."

"Nonsense," said Oliver feebly, "you'll be fine, Dick. But please, don't tell them you saw me! Good luck, Dick. I know you'll be well and happy. We'll meet again." Dick wished Oliver a final good-bye and blessed him. It was the first blessing Oliver had ever been given.

After taking his leave of his little friend, Oliver hurried along the road to London. When he had traveled five miles, he saw a sign that told him it was seventy miles to London. He dodged behind bushes whenever he heard a sound, afraid he'd be caught. He thought of London—that great, noisy, crowded city—not even Mr. Bumble could find him there!

Oliver felt confident as he walked—he had a shirt, a crust of bread, two pairs of socks, and even a penny that Mr. Sowerberry had given him once after a funeral. He stopped occasionally for water at houses along the way. He slept at night and walked during the day. Soon, his feet were blistered and he was very tired. London seemed as far away as ever. He was afraid to beg in some villages, as there were signs that declared that beggars would be imprisoned. If not for a kind woman and an equally kind man, he might have perished on the king's highway. These people gave him bread and cheese and whatever else they could. He had never met people who took pity on a poor orphan before.

On the seventh morning since he'd left the Sowerberry house, Oliver limped into the small town of Barnet. He didn't even have the strength to beg. Suddenly, he noticed a boy approaching him. The boy gave him a cheery hello. Oliver took in the boy's appearance. Truly, he was the oddest-looking youth,

FS-17020 Oliver Twist (retold)

quite the filthiest he could possibly be. Odder yet was that he had the manner of a man, not a child. His face was ordinary enough, but he was short, with bowlegs and tiny, sharp, ugly eyes. He wore a hat lightly on his head, and a man's coat. At about four-feet-six, he was a swaggering, confident mass of dirt.

"Hello, there, me boy," he said in a friendly, matter-of-fact manner. "What are you doing here?"

Oliver could barely hold back the tears. "I've been on the road for seven days," he confessed, "and I'm hungry and tired." Hearing that, the young man helped Oliver to his feet and took him for a meal. They had bread and ham and something to drink.

"Going to London?" the strange boy asked. Oliver shook his head yes. "Got a place to stay or money?" Oliver shook his head no.

"Well," the young man said, "my name is Jack Dawkins, but my friends call me 'the Artful Dodger.' I know an old gentleman who will help you out. And, as luck—your good luck, that is—would have it, I'm going to London too."

FS-17020 Oliver Twist (retold)

Name _____

1. Oliver had withstood many beatings during his young life. Why did he finally decide to run away?

   _____

   _____

2. Do you think Oliver did the right thing by running away? Why or why not? _____

   _____

3. Dick seemed almost happy that he was dying. Why did he have this attitude?

   _____

   _____

4. Why do you think the Artful Dodger is being so friendly to Oliver?

   _____

   _____

5. What do you think Oliver will find in London? What do you think he expects to find? _____

   _____

6. If you were entering a huge city for the first time, what are five things you would do immediately?

   1. _____   2. _____   3. _____

   4. _____   5. _____

FS-17020 Oliver Twist (retold)

CHAPTER 5

THE OLD GENTLEMAN

Oliver had never seen a more dirty or wretched place than the one to which the Dodger guided him. The street was narrow and muddy and the air was filled with unpleasant odors. Although it was late at night, children, in what seemed like great heaps, were outdoors, running about and screaming. Men and women, drunken and filthy, were spilling out of doorways, and disreputable men were cautiously emerging from the depths of somewhere. Oliver thought of turning and running, but they had reached the end of their journey. The Dodger drew Oliver into a passage. The Dodger whistled. A voice replied, "Now, then!" to which the Dodger answered in some sort of code, "Plummy and slam!"

After passing a man's inspection, the pair entered a room whose walls and ceiling were covered with dirt and grime. Within this room was a withered old man with matted red hair. "This here's Fagin," the Dodger said. Oliver looked around. A number of silk handkerchiefs were hanging around the room and a few sacks lay on the floor. Several boys no older than the Dodger sat around a table and jumped up to welcome Oliver. They took his cap and emptied his pockets. Oliver ate and washed.

"We're glad to have you here," said the merry old gentleman. Oliver's luck seemed to have turned for the better. Tired after his meal, he was lifted onto one of the sacks, where he quickly fell asleep.

The next day Oliver awoke and soon found himself watching Fagin. He noticed the old man removing a small box from beneath the floor.

"What are you looking at?" the old man growled. Then, as quickly as he was angered, he became his sweet self that Oliver had seen the night before. "This is my life's savings," he said gently. The box disappeared, seemingly before Oliver's very eyes.

Soon, some of the young boys whom Oliver met the night before entered. One of them was Charley Bates.

"How did it go today?" asked Fagin. "Did you work hard?"

"Hard as nails," reported Bates.

FS-17020 Oliver Twist (retold)

"And what have you for me?" he asked the Dodger.

"Two pocketbooks," answered the boy. "Lined, too, and good workmanship." The old man laughed.

Later, Fagin and the boys played a curious game. The old man stuffed many items in his pockets and the boys removed them. If he felt them removing anything, the game ended and had to begin all over again. Then it was Oliver's turn. Fagin asked him to remove a handkerchief from his pocket. Oliver did as he was told.

"Is it gone?" asked Fagin. "Here it is," replied Oliver. The old man was delighted. "You're a clever boy," he declared.

Meanwhile, a couple of young ladies called to see the young men. Both girls had messy hair and clothing that was none too clean. They weren't pretty girls but were stout and hearty. Their names were Nancy and Betsy.

Oliver played the game every day. He was getting better and better at it and did want to please Fagin. One day both the Dodger and Charley Bates came home empty-handed. For this failure, Fagin knocked the both of them down the stairs.

Oliver was longing to go outside. The Dodger and Charley Bates took him with them into the streets. They had passed shops and seen many people when the Dodger stopped short. "There's a prime plant," he said, looking at a distinguished older gentleman walking near them. Oliver didn't understand, but was horrified to see the Dodger plunge his hand into the gentleman's pocket! He withdrew a silk handkerchief and began to run fast as lightning with Charley at his side. Suddenly, Oliver understood it all: the game, the goods the boys brought home, the watches, the jewels, and most of all, he understood what Fagin was! Oliver, too, began to run, but the police soon caught him. "Is this the thief?" an officer asked the gentleman.

"I'm not sure," said the man truthfully. "Please, sir, it wasn't me," begged Oliver. "It was those other boys." But Oliver was roughly dragged down the streets by the police. The boys watched in triumph. They had gotten away clean!

Name _____

1. Why was Fagin so nice to Oliver? _____

   _____

   _____

   _____

2. What do you think the Dodger meant when he called the man on the street "a prime plant"?
   What would be another expression to describe the man? _____

   _____

   _____

   _____

3. Did you know what Fagin and the boys were doing before Oliver found out? If yes, how did you
   know? Why do you think Oliver didn't know? _____

   _____

   _____

   _____

4. Why did Fagin have the boys play the game with the
   handkerchiefs? _____

   _____

   _____

   _____

5. We know that Oliver was innocent. Pretend you're
   Oliver and are given a chance to explain what really
   happened. Write a note to explain. _____

   _____

   _____

   _____

   _____

   _____

   _____

   _____

          FS-17020 Oliver Twist (retold)

CHAPTER 6

JUSTICE PREVAILS

At the police station Oliver learned that the robbery victim was a Mr. Brownlow. The frightened boy had been roughly rushed to the station, beaten severely on the way, then tossed into a filthy cell. Mr. Brownlow followed to identify the perpetrator. He tried to speak to the policeman.

"I-I'm really not certain that this was the boy who stole my handkerchief," Mr. Brownlow declared. "Something about him touches me. I don't know what it is. I almost feel as though I've seen his face before. I wish to drop the charges."

"Can't do that," the officer shook his head. "You've got to appear before Mr. Fang. He's the magistrate, and he doesn't put up with nonsense."

Mr. Brownlow appeared before the magistrate.

"Who are you?" Mr. Fang demanded. "What crime did you commit? We deal harshly with criminals, be warned!"

"Why, I'm the man who was robbed, but I'm not really sure that this boy did it. Everything happened so fast. Everyone yelled, 'Stop thief!' and this boy was running. He may be innocent."

Mr. Fang interrupted. "How dare you bully a magistrate!" he bellowed, then turned to Oliver, who had been brought in and told to stand before Mr. Fang.

"What is your name?" he yelled at Oliver.

The trembling boy was so frightened he couldn't even utter his own name. Mr. Fang looked at him disgustedly.

"Are there witnesses against this boy?"

A man stepped forward. "Sir," he said timidly, "the gentleman, Mr. Brownlow, I believe he is called, was buying a book at my bookstall just before this occurred. I saw the whole thing. This boy is innocent."

"Then get him out of here!" roared Mr. Fang.

Oliver found it difficult to stand up. Was he truly free? He had been certain he was about to fulfill the prophecy about him declared when he was at the workhouse: that he would hang on the gallows.

          FS-17020 Oliver Twist (retold)

"Case dismissed!" shouted Mr. Fang. "A colossal waste of time! I should lock you all up!"

Weakly, Oliver left the police station.

"There's something about him," repeated Mr. Brownlow to himself. "Something familiar." As he, too, left the station he was dismayed to see frail, pale little Oliver Twist lying on the pavement. His face was white and his whole body was trembling uncontrollably. Mr. Brownlow summoned a coach.

"Driver, help me with this boy. I shall take him home and make him well. There's no time to lose." He saw the bookseller, a kind and honest man, standing next to him. "May I come too?" the bookseller asked.

"Quickly, man, there's no time to lose!" Mr. Brownlow ordered the coachman to hurry. They thundered down the road. As concerned as Mr. Brownlow was about the boy's health, he could not shake the nagging feeling that he knew him, or someone like him.

FS-17020 Oliver Twist (retold)

Name _____

1. Why was Oliver treated so cruelly when the police caught him?
   _____

2. What kind of person do you think Mr. Fang was?
   _____

3. If you were accused of stealing something and were innocent, how would you persuade the police that you didn't do it? _____
   _____
   _____

4. Why did the bookseller come forward to be a witness?
   _____
   _____

5. What would you do if you were a witness to a crime?
   _____
   _____
   _____

6. How do you think Fagin will feel about Oliver's disappearance?
   _____
   _____
   _____

FS-17020 Oliver Twist (retold)

CHAPTER 7

HEAVEN

By the time the coach reached Mr. Brownlow's house near a town called Pentonville, he was sorely afraid for Oliver's life.

"Mrs. Bedwin! Come please! I need your help!" Mr. Brownlow called to his housekeeper.

The kindly housekeeper quickly prepared a bed for the ragged young stranger, who did appear to be on the verge of his demise. Oliver was carefully deposited into the bed, where he slept for many days. He was feverish and unconscious, but all the while tended by members of the household.

Finally, Oliver woke up and saw Mrs. Bedwin sitting by his bed.

"My word!" exclaimed Mrs. Bedwin with delight, "I thought you were going to leave us for certain." She beamed.

Oliver sat up in bed. "Is this heaven?" he asked. Mr. Brownlow chuckled, "No, young man, just an ordinary house." But the soft, clean bed and people with care showing on their faces was heaven as far as Oliver was concerned. Life could not be this sweet.

The family doctor was sent for to examine Oliver. The doctor prescribed food and rest as Oliver's treatment for a full recovery.

Oliver grew stronger each day. He was soon carried down to the housekeeper's room. There, he couldn't help but notice a portrait of an attractive young woman on the wall.

"Who is that lady?" Oliver asked, pointing to the portrait. "She looks like someone I know, but I can't think who for the life of me."

Mr. Brownlow began to explain but suddenly stopped. Someone the lad knew? The portrait's features were the same as Oliver's. It was his face!

"Why," suggested an astonished Mr. Brownlow, "this portrait is the living copy of your face!" Hearing that, Oliver fainted.

Meanwhile, the reader may ask, "How about Fagin and his gang?"

The Dodger and Charley Bates scurried back to Fagin's like two rats. They had both had their fun for the day.

"Where's the boy?" Fagin shouted.

"We lost him," said Bates. "He's with the law by now, I venture."

© Frank Schaffer Publications, Inc.

Furious, Fagin grabbed a pot of beer and hurled it at the boys. It missed its mark, instead landing right in the face of a most disreputable character named Bill Sikes, who was just walking in.

"Hey! I'll give you what for, old man!" he shouted. He was accompanied by a man quite as disgusting-looking as himself.

Fagin was obviously frightened of Bill Sikes, who was a sight in soiled coat and breeches and a dirty handkerchief around his neck.

"What's going on, you dirty old rascal? You seem to be in bad humor." Sikes settled down in the room.

"It's that boy I was training," growled Fagin. "It looks like he's been nabbed by the police. He could say things dangerous to us and our business."

As they were talking, Nancy and Betsy, the two young women who often frequented Fagin's dwelling, came in. They were in time to hear Bill Sikes agree with Fagin.

"That's the truth," agreed Sikes. "We must send someone to the police station to find out what happened to the boy. It has to be someone innocent-looking, so the police won't suspect a thing."

Sikes and Fagin looked at the girls. "Not me," insisted Betsy. "I won't go. Police stations make me feel sick."

"I'll go," said the agreeable Nancy and she cheerfully set out for the police station.

Soon, Nancy was at the police station, and what a performance she gave! Blubbering, she enlisted the sympathy of an officer.

"Please, sir," she sniveled, "that's my little brother they've got there. I've been so worried. Where is he?"

The officer lost no time in telling Nancy exactly where Oliver had been taken.

Nancy returned to Fagin's lair and presented him with the news. Sikes promptly left. Fagin gathered his treasures about him and announced to his gang of boys, "We're going to change our residence for now. And boys, leave no stone unturned until you find that ungrateful little beggar. Then I'll give him what he deserves."

FS-17020 Oliver Twist (retold)

Name _____

1. How could the portrait look just like Oliver? Who do you think the woman might be?

_____

_____

2. Why did Oliver think he must be in heaven? _____

_____

_____

3. Was it a lucky coincidence that Oliver and Mr. Brownlow met? Write about a lucky coincidence that happened to you. _____

_____

_____

_____

_____

4. What did Fagin think Oliver might do to cause him trouble?

_____

_____

5. Why did Fagin gather his treasures and leave his hideout?

_____

_____

FS-17020 Oliver Twist (retold)

CHAPTER 8

ALL IS LOST

"Where is the portrait of the lady, sir?" Oliver asked Mr. Brownlow upon regaining consciousness. The wall was empty. The kind old gentleman put an arm around the orphan.

"It seemed to upset you, Oliver, so I had it taken down."

Oliver didn't protest.

"Now, my boy, I'd like to hear all about the life of the young man I'm entertaining." But to the old man's surprise, Oliver began to weep, quite unprepared to discuss the details of his horrible life. As he began to regain control and speak to Mr. Brownlow, however, a visitor appeared.

"Oh, it's my friend Mr. Grimwig. Welcome, and come meet Oliver Twist." Mr. Grimwig looked Oliver up and down distrustfully.

"So, that's the boy, is it?" he inquired.

"Yes, and a good-looking boy he is, isn't he?"

Mr. Grimwig was not to be won over by Oliver so quickly.

"Is he?" he asked. "I don't see any difference in boys. There are two kinds of boys, mealy boys and beef-faced boys."

"And which is Oliver?" asked the host.

"Mealy," responded Mr. Grimwig. "And when are we going to hear the remarkable adventures of Oliver Twist?"

"Tomorrow," answered Mr. Brownlow, "when he and I are alone."

Mr. Brownlow told Oliver he'd see him in the morning. After the boy took leave of them, Mr. Grimwig said, "He's not to be trusted, I tell you. He's a thief."

Just then some books were delivered from the very bookstall where Mr. Brownlow had been a victim of robbery. "Wait!" he called out. "I want to send money to the bookseller and return some books I don't want." But the delivery boy was gone.

Mr. Grimwig got a gleam in his eye. "Let's test the boy," he challenged. "Give him the money and the books and send him to the bookseller. I'll wager he'll take it and return to his thieving friends." Mr. Brownlow was hesitant, but agreed. He summoned Oliver and told him of his mission.

"Am I not to come back?" asked a worried Oliver.

FS-17020 Oliver Twist (retold)

"Of course you're to come back, my boy," said Mr. Brownlow. Oliver then went on his way.

Mrs. Bedwin cautioned, "I don't like it, sir. Out there alone, I'm afraid something dreadful will happen to little Oliver."

"Don't worry, he'll be back in twenty minutes." Mr. Brownlow informed her.

"You don't really expect to ever see him again, do you?" smirked Mr. Grimwig. "He'll take your money, the books, the excellent clothing that you gave him and go back to his old life."

It grew very dark, and the two men sat silently, one hoping the boy would soon return, the other certain he never would.

Meanwhile, Oliver was heading toward the bookseller's on his errand. Not being familiar with the streets, he took a wrong turn and was shocked to be suddenly embraced by a tearful young woman.

"Oh, my dear brother," she cried, "how could you leave us?" A crowd gathered. "Oh, he's taken up evil ways," said Nancy, pretending to be Oliver's sister. Suddenly, Bill Sikes emerged from a tavern, knocked Oliver on the head with the books he was carrying and carted him away.

"That'll teach the scoundrel," the crowd roared with approval. Bill Sikes dragged the unconscious Oliver to Fagin's lair.

"He's back!" yelled the Dodger, who proceeded to search the pockets of Oliver's fine clothes. He and Charley Bates took the money that Mr. Brownlow had given the boy to pay the bookseller.

"Please," begged Oliver, as he awoke, "send the books back." He tried to escape but was held by Fagin. The old man began to beat the boy, but Nancy came to his defense.

"Leave him alone, you wicked old man!" she shouted and grabbed the club that Fagin was using on Oliver. She threw it in the fire. Bill Sikes grabbed Nancy's arm and she fainted.

"Throw him in that room!" ordered Fagin, and poor Oliver slept there all night.

© Frank Schaffer Publications, Inc.

FS-17020 Oliver Twist (retold)

Name _____

1. Do you think Mr. Brownlow did the right thing by listening to Mr. Grimwig's advice? Why or why not? _____

   _____

2. How could Oliver have avoided being recaptured by the gang?

   _____

   _____

3. Nancy seemed at first to go along with anything that Fagin wanted. Why did she turn on him when he was beating Oliver?

   _____

   _____

4. What do you think the author was trying to tell us about Nancy's character? _____

   _____

   _____

5. When he first met Oliver, Fagin treated him with kindness. When they met again, he was cruel to him. Why did Fagin change? Which Fagin is the real one? _____

   _____

   _____

FS-17020 Oliver Twist (retold)

CHAPTER 9

THE BEADLE

Mr. Bumble strolled down the road on his way to see Mrs. Mann.

"Oh, drat, what does the beadle want at this time of the morning?" Mrs. Mann asked herself as she saw him approaching. But when he arrived, she was all smiles.

"I'm taking two of the paupers to London regarding a settlement," he declared importantly. "And how are your little boys?"

"They're all well, except that stubborn little Dick. Well, two others have died, but that nasty boy hangs on to life. He's no better."

"Bring him to me," commanded the beadle, "so I may look at him."

Dick came in. His cheeks were pale and sunken. His eyes shone bright and huge in his tiny face.

"Look the gentleman in the eye, you horrible boy," she demanded.

"Well, what do you want, boy?" the beadle asked.

"I should like, would like . . ."

Mrs. Mann exploded. "Does he think he actually wants for something? He gets nothing but the best of care!"

"Now, now, kind lady," comforted the beadle. "Out with it, boy, what do you want?"

"Before I am laid in the ground, sir, I want someone to write a message for Oliver Twist, and give it to him when I am gone so he'll know I was glad to die young. Now I'll be in heaven with my sister."

"The nerve!" yelled Mrs. Mann. "It's that evil Oliver Twist, poisoning the minds of these wretches! Get out of here!" Dick walked out. Mrs. Mann was visibly upset.

"There, there, it's all right, kind lady," soothed the beadle. And he took his leave to go to London.

Having arrived in London, Mr. Bumble saw an amazing sight, a poster offering a reward for information leading to the whereabouts of one Oliver Twist, "absconded or enticed from his home at Pentonville." There followed a complete description of Oliver and the

FS-17020 Oliver Twist (retold)

address and name of the person who was interested in his location. Mr. Bumble was immediately on his way to Pentonville.

"Mr. Brownlow," he began, when he was admitted to the house, "I know Oliver Twist. He is the son of vicious and low parents. From the day of his birth he displayed treachery, ingratitude, and malice."

"I don't believe it!" exclaimed the old gentleman. But Mr. Bumble produced documents proving he was who he claimed to be. Mr. Brownlow gave Mr. Bumble the reward sadly and the beadle left.

"Mrs. Bedwin," he told the housekeeper, "I fear that young Oliver has fooled us. He is not what he seemed to be, but rather is the foundling of a low and vile family."

"I'll never believe it," said the housekeeper tearfully. "I know the boy. He is good and . . ."

"Mrs. Bedwin, you are never to mention that boy's name in this house again," Mr. Brownlow declared forcefully. "We will forget we ever opened our home and our hearts to him. You may leave the room, Mrs. Bedwin. And never forget, I am in earnest."

Fortunately for Oliver, in his misery, he was spared the knowledge that in Mr. Brownlow's happy home there was sadness as great as his own.

FS-17020 Oliver Twist (retold)

Name _____

1. Why do you think Dick wanted a letter to be written to Oliver?

   _____

   _____

2. Write the letter that you think Dick would have written.

   Dearest Oliver,

   _____

   _____

   _____

   _____

   Your friend, Dick

3. Why didn't Mrs. Mann look forward to the visit of the beadle?

   _____

   _____

   _____

   _____

   _____

4. Why were Mr. Bumble and Mrs. Mann so shocked and angry at Dick's request?

   _____

   _____

   _____

   _____

5. Mr. Bumble said terrible things about Oliver when he went to see Mr. Brownlow. Do you think he meant it? Why or why not?

   _____

   _____

   _____

   _____

   _____

   _____

   _____

FS-17020 Oliver Twist (retold)

CHAPTER 10

IN THE GANG'S CLUTCHES

Oliver was constantly afraid, but Fagin seemed to have mellowed toward him a bit. "Don't forget," he reminded Oliver, "the hangman is just around the corner. If you betray me, I'll see you get blamed for enough to get you hanged. You'd better come around."

Fagin wanted his quick-learning former pupil to take up the trade, but Oliver refused. How odd that this lad, abused all his life, had a sense of right and wrong!

At first, Oliver was locked up, but after about a week, he was allowed the run of the house. He was even allowed to polish the Dodger's boots.

"Hey, you'd better get back in with Fagin, you know," advised the Dodger as his boots were being done.

"I'd rather not," said Oliver, "I'd rather go. Anyway, you both abandoned me to be caught by the police."

FS-17020 Oliver Twist (retold)

"Aw, now, Oliver, we had to do that, you know. We'd have been stupid to stick around. You'd better face it—you'll have to do what Fagin wants pretty soon. Fagin can be a nice old gentleman when you do his bidding."

A boy entered who Oliver didn't know, Tom Chitling by name.

"I've just come out of the prison. I was there for six weeks," he almost bragged.

Oliver was no longer alone, but usually had the company of the other boys or of Fagin himself. Fagin regaled the crew with stories of his criminal life, which the boys properly appreciated. Poor Oliver didn't realize that Fagin had a plan—he had made the boy so lonely for company that even that of Fagin and the other boys was now welcome to Oliver. Fagin believed it was just a matter of time before he had Oliver living the despicable life of a pickpocket.

One damp, foul night Fagin made his way toward Bill Sikes's place to hatch a plan. Nancy was with Bill. Fagin and Bill discussed a robbery.

"Have some brandy," offered Bill, but Fagin hesitated. It could be poisoned, he thought.

"Nancy, get out," ordered Bill cruelly. But Fagin, smiling, asked the girl to stay.

"Surely you can trust Nancy," he reminded Bill.

"That boy, that Oliver," bragged Fagin. "He's almost mine. Just a little while longer and I'll have him begging to work for me."

"What's so grand about him?" asked Bill. "There are fifty others for the taking."

"He's worth the fifty," replied Fagin. "He has remarkable talent for our trade."

"Maybe, but you can't trust him. When we do the place at Chertsey he has to be along. Once he does a robbery with us, he's ours for life. Bring him to me." Fagin agreed enthusiastically.

Bill ended the meeting by drinking himself into a stupor.

Nancy was there all the while. Fagin watched her. Surely they could trust her, in spite of her liking for the boy.

When Fagin returned to his place, he wanted to tell Oliver what his future was to be. But the boy was fast asleep, and Fagin decided it wasn't worth waking him up. He stared at the boy. Oliver looked so pale, Fagin thought, as though he were dead.

"Not now," croaked Fagin in a whisper, "Not now. Tomorrow."

Name _____

1. Why was it impossible for Oliver to escape his captors?

   _____

   _____

2. Why was Fagin so determined to have Oliver become a thief?

   _____

   _____

3. Do you think Fagin and Sikes trusted each other? Explain.

   _____

   _____

4. There is a saying, "There is honor among thieves." Is this true with Fagin's gang? Why or why

   not? _____

   _____

5. The boys who lived with and worked for Fagin all seem to be very loyal to him. Why? _____

   _____

   _____

6. Who do you think seems more dangerous,
   Bill Sikes or Fagin? Explain your answer.

   _____

   _____

   _____

   _____

   _____

   _____

FS-17020 Oliver Twist (retold)

CHAPTER 11

OLIVER BETRAYED

The next morning, Oliver awoke to find a new pair of shoes by his bed. As he put them on, Fagin issued him a warning.

"See here, you're going to Bill Sikes's place today. He'll take charge of you. Don't think of crossing him; he's a bad one. Take heed, Oliver, take heed and do Bill's bidding, lest you be sorry. I'm sorry to tell you that Bill Sikes doesn't have my kind nature. Here, while you're waiting for Nancy to take you to Bill's, read this book." He tossed a book at Oliver, who was most distressed to see that it was all about infamous criminals and their careers. The details were gruesome.

Nancy fetched Oliver and transported him to Bill's.

"Remember, you mind Bill so you don't make him mad," she cautioned.

Oliver noticed that she looked a bit nervous. The boy sensed that he was in for a bad time at the hands of Bill Sikes. He thought of running away.

"Don't worry," smiled Nancy, but she looked awfully pale. "You'll come to no harm. Look," she said seriously, "I did my best for you, but it's no good." She didn't tell him that she'd already been beaten for defending him.

They arrived at Bill Sikes's place, who made no pretense of being nice. "So, you brought him," said Sikes. "Did he give you any trouble?" Nancy shook her head no.

"Now," began Sikes, "see this here gun?" He pressed a pistol to Oliver's head. "You're never to speak to me unless I tell you to. Do you know what will happen to you if you do?"

Oliver was terrified. Nancy said, lest Oliver not understand the threat, "He means to do you in if you talk to him, Oliver."

It was a damp, windy morning as Sikes and Oliver set out. They made their way to Smithfield, which was a hubbub of activity early in the morning. It was market day, and the town was filled with unsavory characters. Oliver saw unshaven, squalid, unwashed, and dirty figures everywhere.

"Don't lollygag about," growled Bill. "We have a way to go, Lazylegs!" At this pronouncement, he jerked at Oliver's wrist.

Sikes stopped a man and asked him for a ride in his wagon.

"Is that your boy?" the man asked.

"Yes, he's my boy," Sikes answered, putting his hand in his pocket to remind Oliver of the presence of the pistol.

They traveled for a while, then got out. Sikes found other rides for them. Oliver was sorely tempted to cry for help but was afraid for his life and the lives of those they met.

Oliver trudged with Sikes through mud and darkness, through gloomy land and cold open wastes. Finally, they reached the foot of a bridge, and Oliver saw water below them.

Oh no, he thought with icy fear, *he's brought me here to murder me!* He was about to throw himself on the ground and struggle for his young life when he saw a ruined, decayed house looming in front of them. It seemed uninhabited. Upon reaching the house, Sikes raised the latch and passed through the door, Oliver in tow. They were greeted by Barney and Toby, who soon forced Oliver to eat and drink.

"Come on, you've had enough," Sikes growled. They all set out, with Oliver between them. Soon, they approached a house in the town of Chertsey. It became clear to Oliver. They were there to rob it!

"No, sir, please!" Oliver begged. "Please let me go!"

Sikes, out of patience with the boy, cocked his pistol.

"Leave him be," said Toby. "Let's get to the business at hand."

Sikes unlocked a narrow window to the pantry and removed the shutter. He ordered Oliver to go through it, then come around and open the front door for them. Suddenly, Sikes saw something at the doorway of the room and yelled to Oliver, "Come back!" But from the doorway came a noise, smoke, and a crash. Sikes fired his gun, reached in through the window, and dragged a bleeding Oliver away.

FS-17020 Oliver Twist (retold)

Name _____

1. What did Fagin and Sikes plan for Oliver? _____

_____

_____

2. How did Sikes threaten Oliver? _____

_____

3. Why didn't Nancy continue to protect Oliver? _____

_____

4. When they reached the bridge, what did Oliver think Sikes was going to do to him? Why did he think that? _____

_____

5. Why did the burglars need Oliver at the house? _____

_____

6. How did the burglary go wrong? _____

_____

7. What happened to Oliver? Why did Sikes take him with them instead of leaving him behind?

_____

_____

FS-17020 Oliver Twist (retold)

CHAPTER 12

OLD SALLY

Mrs. Corney, the matron of the workhouse where Oliver was born, was about to sit down and enjoy her tea. But before she could, there was a rap at the door.

"Oh, it's Mr. Bumble!" she exclaimed. "Please come in!"

Mr. Bumble made himself at home. "You have cats," he remarked.

"Yes, I rather fancy them. And mine are so fond of their home."

"Ma'am, any cat would be fond to live with you," he smiled.

Mrs. Corney blushed with embarrassment. Just then, they were interrupted by an old female pauper.

"If you please, mistress, old Sally's going fast!" she reported.

"What's that to me?" inquired Mrs. Corney angrily. "I can't keep her alive, can I?"

"No, mistress, but when she's not having the fits, she says she has something she must tell you."

Mrs. Corney asked Mr. Bumble to wait for her. She went to the dying woman's bed.

Suddenly, old Sally sat upright and stared ahead of her.

"I have to tell her! Now, listen to me. Long ago, in this very room, a young woman gave birth to a baby, then died."

"What about it?" cried Mrs. Corney, somewhat curious.

"I stole it from her," sobbed old Sally. "It was gold! She showed it to me hanging around her neck. Perhaps if they'd known about it, they would have treated her better. And her tiny son. If he's dead too, it's my fault! She trusted me."

"If they'd known what? What was the boy's name?" demanded the matron.

"They called him 'Oliver.' The gold I stole was . . ."

And with that last utterance she fell back, stone dead.

"She had nothing to tell after all," said Mrs. Corney, walking away.

FS-17020 Oliver Twist (retold)

Name _____

1. How did Mr. Bumble and the matron of the workhouse, Mrs. Corney, feel about each other? _____

   _____

2. Why do you think the author had old Sally die before she could reveal the secret she'd been carrying for years? _____

   _____

   _____

3. What do you think the piece of gold might be? How will it influence Oliver's life?

   _____

   _____

   _____

4. Why do you think old Sally wanted to confess before she died?

   _____

   _____

5. Dickens often interrupts his own story and takes the reader to another scene. Why do you think he left the scene where Oliver was shot and shifted to the death of old Sally?

   _____

   _____

   _____

FS-17020 Oliver Twist (retold)

CHAPTER 13

A GATHERING OF THIEVES

Dawkins (also known as the Dodger), Bates, and Chitling were playing cards. The bell rang and the Dodger went to answer it. It was Toby Crackit, looking worn and hungry.

"Where are Bill and the boy?" asked Fagin.

"I don't know," answered Toby honestly. "The robbery went bad. The boy got shot, and the very ones we were trying to rob set everyone on us. Bill left the boy in a ditch. He was bleeding something fierce."

"You idiot!" Fagin roared. "That boy is valuable!" With that, he left the house.

Traveling quickly through the familiar streets, Fagin stopped at a tavern. It was a smoke-filled place crowded with Fagin's type of people: low, vicious, and criminal.

"I'm looking for Monks," he told the landlord.

"He'll come by soon, of that I'm sure, Mr. Fagin. Will you wait?"

"No," replied Fagin, "but when he comes, tell him I'll see him tomorrow."

Fagin went to Bill Sikes's place. Sikes wasn't there, but Nancy was.

"Well, my girl," smiled Fagin, "Where's Bill? And the boy?"

Nancy lashed out at the old man. "I don't know where Bill is, and I hope Oliver is lying dead in a ditch. He's better off there than with the likes of you!"

He suddenly thought that the girl might know more than she should about his business, but Fagin dismissed the idea.

Fagin returned home through the dark and dank streets. He was aware of someone dogging his footsteps. It was Monks.

"The whole thing went bad," complained Monks.

"And what about the boy?" asked Fagin.

"It was that blasted girl's fault for favoring him!" Monks spat out. "She should be throttled!"

"It's true she did favor him, but she's harmless," insisted Fagin.

Suddenly, Fagin saw the shadow of a woman pass along the wall. They both looked throughout the house, but no one was there.

Name _____

1. It doesn't seem that Monks was involved in the attempted burglary, so why do you think Fagin sought him out?

   _____

   _____

   _____

2. In a good story, the main character experiences lots of high and low points. Fill in the chart below that tells about the characters in the story so far and how the main character's life has progressed.

   Main character: _____ (protagonist or hero)

   Main enemy of that character: _____ (antagonist)

   People who influence the main character's life: _____

   _____ _____ _____ _____ _____

   Good things that happen to the hero: _____

   _____

   _____

   Bad things that happen to the hero: _____

   _____

   _____

FS-17020 Oliver Twist (retold)

CHAPTER 14

LOVE AND THE BEADLE

Mr. Bumble was growing impatient. Mrs. Corney had left him by himself for quite a while. The woman was a saint, he thought, helping a dying woman when she could have been entertaining him!

While waiting, he thought it would be an excellent time to survey Mrs. Corney's property. Looking around to make sure nobody was observing him, he began to rummage through a chest of drawers.

"The woman does seem to own a few nice things," he mused aloud. "Hello, what's this?" The beadle unearthed a locked box. He shook it. A delightful metallic sound, much like money, greeted him.

That very sound seemed to make up his mind for him! "I'll do it!" he declared.

Mrs. Corney returned, flustered. "Oh, what a bother these paupers are! Excuse my absence, kind sir." She smiled sweetly.

"Is there something wrong, dear?" Mr. Bumble inquired. "You seem frightened." Mrs. Corney assured him that nothing was wrong.

"Mrs. Corney," informed the beadle, "Mr. Slout, the workhouse master, is very old and near death, you know. The almost certain choice to fill his position would be none other than I."

He cleared his throat and continued. "Your lovely place here is big enough for two, and I thought . . ."

"Say no more, Mr. Bumble. We shall, of course, be married. And when we are, I'll have something to tell you. It's what was vexing me."

"Surely, my love, you can tell me now that we're engaged," suggested Mr. Bumble, but the future Mrs. Bumble would not be moved. Mr. Bumble took his leave.

On his way home, he passed the undertaker's place and went right in. No one seemed to be about. He rapped on the counter several times, but no one came. He decided to take a peek into the little parlor that was in the back of the shop.

"My stars!" the beadle exclaimed when he saw none other than the Sowerberrys' employees, Noah Claypole and Charlotte, lolling about the room. Noah was sitting on the table leaning back on his arms in a lazy manner. Charlotte was digging into a barrel of oysters.

FS-17020 Oliver Twist (retold)

"How glad I am that the Sowerberrys went out to tea. We have the whole place to ourselves!" said Noah gleefully.

"Don't you want any oysters, Noah?" asked Charlotte.

"No, my dear, they're not to my taste, but I enjoy watching you eat them. Come over here, Charlotte, and I'll kiss you," he promised.

"What!" exclaimed Mr. Bumble as he burst onto the scene.

"Say that again, sir!" Noah quickly placed his feet on the floor, and Charlotte hid her face in her apron.

"Mr. Bumble, sir, it's not my fault," whimpered Noah. "She chases me around and kisses me all the time, and I don't even want her to!"

"Silence!" commanded Mr. Bumble. "Now close up the shop. When your master returns, tell him there's a coffin needed at Mrs. Corney's for an old woman." He began to mumble to himself, "Kissing! What have the lower classes sunk to! Sin and wickedness, I say!"

He strode away from the dreadful scene, nose in the air.

FS-17020 Oliver Twist (retold)

Name _____

1. Why was Mrs. Corney flustered when she joined Mr. Bumble?

    _____

    _____

2. Do you think Mr. Bumble truly cared for Mrs. Corney? Why did he want to marry her? _____

    _____

    _____

3. Why was Mr. Bumble going to the undertaker's? _____

    _____

    _____

4. What shocked Mr. Bumble? _____

    _____

5. Charlotte and Noah made a big fuss over the oysters. What do you think was so special about
    them? _____

    _____

    _____

6. Noah was glad that the Sowerberrys were gone so he could do
    whatever he wished. What was wrong about what he and
    Charlotte did? _____

    _____

    _____

    _____

7. How do you feel about Noah? How do you think he should
    end up in the story? _____

    _____

    _____

    _____

    _____

FS-17020 Oliver Twist (retold)

CHAPTER 15

FOUND AGAIN

And what about dear little Oliver? As the thieves were running from the law, carrying the bleeding boy with them, their burden was slowing them down.

"Let's just leave him here," said Toby, panting. At that, Bill Sikes dropped Oliver over a hedge. His companions kept running. As for the posse that was in hot pursuit, they got tired of the chase and gave up. All of them—Mr. Giles, a butler living in the mansion that was the target of the bungled burglary; Brittles, a handyman; and a tinker whose dogs had aided in tracking the thieves—were worn out.

Oliver lay unconscious in the mud all night. Around daylight, with the rain falling on him and his left arm quite soaked with his own blood, Oliver came to. Somehow he was able to stagger across the fields.

He reached a road and saw a house. As he approached the house, he realized, too late, that it was the one at Chertsey that the gang tried to rob. But what could he do? He was desperate.

The weakened boy rapped at the door, then sank against a pillar.

"I'm telling you," said Giles, "we almost had them and what a fight it would have been! I heard them and I got out of bed. I crept down to face the intruders, and suddenly . . ." Oliver's feeble knock was heard at the door, and the maid, being totally engrossed in Giles's story, screamed.

"It's just a knock at the door," said Giles. He opened the door and beheld Oliver, slumped against the pillar.

"Why, it's a thief. It's the one I shot! He's one of them. I shot him!" shouted Giles.

A young lady, Rose Maylie, who lived in the house, approached. "Why, he's bleeding! Get him into the house. Take him to Giles's room, then take the coach to Chertsey and get the doctor. Hurry!" she commanded.

The doctor came. "What happened? How was he wounded?" asked Dr. Losberne. Giles told him, "He climbed in through the window. I shot him."

The doctor went upstairs to see the thief, then called Rose up.

"Have you seen him?" the doctor asked. "Look."

Rose was amazed to see not a hardened criminal but a small boy.

"Oh, the poor lad. Surely he can't be a criminal," said Rose, as she looked at Oliver with pity.

The doctor pointed out that many boys turn to crime.

FS-17020 Oliver Twist (retold)

"But," insisted Rose, for she had a kind and generous heart, "perhaps if he did do evil things it was because he had no love or care."

"We'll wait until he wakes up and has some strength back, then we will question him about his past," decided the doctor.

When Oliver woke up, he told his sordid life story to Mrs. Maylie (the owner of the house), Rose, and Dr. Losberne. They were horrified to hear it.

Even the doctor wept for poor Oliver. He went downstairs and spoke to Giles and Brittles.

"How is the boy?" Giles asked. Dr. Losberne told them that Oliver's arm was broken.

"See here, you two, can you absolutely swear that this is the boy who came through the small window?" The two understood what the doctor required of them. Giles said, "Well, no, I cannot be perfectly sure it was he." Brittles nodded in agreement.

The next day the police came. "Can you identify this boy?" they asked. "Is he the one who entered your house?" Brittles came forward. "I'm not sure this is the boy," he swore. The police left.

Oliver was once again surrounded by people who cared about him. He was saved again, having stumbled onto good luck. His three new friends vowed to nurse him back to health.

© Frank Schaffer Publications, Inc.

FS-17020 Oliver Twist (retold)

Name _____

1. In what condition was Oliver when he knocked on the Maylies' door? _____
   _____

2. Why didn't his rescuers know immediately that Oliver was a little boy?
   _____
   _____

3. Why would people who were nearly robbed rescue someone they believed to be one of the
   robbers? _____
   _____
   _____

4. If you were Oliver, what would you have thought when you awoke once again in a soft,
   comfortable bed? _____
   _____
   _____

5. We have met many characters in the story of Oliver Twist. Write which ones are your favorites
   and why.

   a. _____
   _____

   b. _____
   _____

   c. _____
   _____

CHAPTER 16

A NEW LIFE

Oliver settled into his new life very well. He healed in time, for he not only had a broken arm but fever as well. Spending the night in the wet mud had not been good for him. He expressed his gratitude toward the ladies often, and they were so happy to have rescued him.

"Oh, dear ladies," he cried, "I only want to serve you with my whole heart and soul!"

"Dear boy," smiled Rose, "we want to take you to the countryside with us so you can get well faster. When you're healed, we'll talk about such things."

One day, Oliver set out in Mrs. Maylie's carriage with Dr. Losberne. As they passed Chertsey Bridge, Oliver turned pale. The doctor was afraid he still was not well. "What's wrong, my boy?" he asked.

"That house!" he pointed out. "That's where they all met!"

The doctor jumped out of the carriage and ran to the house. As he leaned against the door, a small hump-backed man opened it.

"What do you want?" asked the little man. "Have you come to rob or to murder me?"

"Not I, you ridiculous old vampire, but I must know if others came to this house recently to do those very things."

"I've lived in this house alone and mad for many years!" screamed the man, who began to dance around in a rage. "Go away!"

"I'll get what I want from you yet," said the doctor. He threw a coin at the man and left.

Oliver was waiting for him in the carriage. The doctor was disturbed that he couldn't get any information out of the hunchback. There was no way he could be certain that Oliver's story was true.

There was yet another way to find the truth about Oliver, so Dr. Losberne had the driver make haste to the home of Mr. Brownlow. Oliver was beside himself with joy that he might see kind Mr. Brownlow and Mrs. Bedwin again. But as they approached the house, the boy's heart sank. There was a "For Rent" sign on it and it was quite obviously empty.

"Don't lose hope," said Dr. Losberne. "We shall inquire of the neighbors."

He knocked at the house next door. A servant answered. Dr. Losberne asked about Mr. Brownlow.

"Oh, he, his housekeeper, and a friend of his left for the West Indies six weeks ago. They're not expected to return."

Oliver's hopes were dashed, but he had a thought.

"Please, sir, do let's go to the bookseller's. I know how to get there." But Dr. Losberne didn't see the point. "My boy," he said sadly, "no doubt if we went we'd find him gone, or dead. Let's just go home." Oliver was so disappointed that he couldn't let his friends know that he was well and happy.

Rose and Mrs. Maylie kept their word and took Oliver to recover in the country. It was beautiful around the cottage where they stayed. A balmy springtime filled the boy with happy days and peaceful nights. He had never known such happiness.

Rose discovered that Oliver's education had been sadly neglected so she saw to it that he had a tutor to improve his reading and writing. And before Oliver knew it, three blissful months had passed. He grew stronger and happier daily, delighting in doing small tasks for the ladies to show his gratitude. They, in turn, were happy in his company, as he proved to be a kind and gentle lad who showed joy in the simplest pleasures.

Name _____

1. Why do you think Dr. Losberne is suspicious of Oliver's story and wants to check it out?

_____

2. How do you think Dr. Losberne could contact Mr. Brownlow in the West Indies? Remember, telephones and computers had not been invented yet. _____

_____

_____

3. Oliver has known happiness before, just to have it snatched away from him. How might this happen again? Write in detail.

_____

_____

_____

_____

4. Compare and contrast the life that Oliver had with the Maylies and Mr. Brownlow with the one he had with Fagin.

	Fagin	The Maylies and Mr. Brownlow
Kind of House		
Clothing		
Food		
Care		

FS-17020 Oliver Twist (retold)

CHAPTER 17

ROSE MAYLIE

The summer quickly came and went. One day as Oliver was strolling with Rose and Mrs. Maylie, Rose became ill. She was put to bed with a fever. Mrs. Maylie called to Oliver.

"Dear, please take this letter to Chertsey so the express rider can take it to the doctor," Mrs. Maylie told him. "This other letter can wait." Oliver saw it was addressed to a "Harry Maylie."

Oliver sped through the fields on his four-mile trip as quickly as he could. After depositing the letter, he collided with a tall man in a cloak.

"Hah! What the devil's this!" the man snarled.

Oliver quickly apologized. "I'm sorry, sir, I was in such a hurry!"

"Rot you! Curses be upon you!" said the man, who was in such a state that he quickly fell to the ground in a fit. Oliver called for help and the man was taken to the inn. Oliver ran home eager to know about Rose.

"Rose is at a crossroads," he was told. "She will either begin to get well or die tonight." Oliver went to the cemetery and prayed. Days passed. Rose did not die, but she did not get better either. Then one day, Dr. Losberne left Rose's room and called everyone together.

"She will live and be well!" he announced. The household was joyful again. The next day Oliver was stopped on the road by a gentleman he did not know. The gentleman asked about Rose's health.

"She is quite well, sir," Oliver answered. Giles came along and called the stranger "Mr. Harry." Harry Maylie was about twenty-five years old, of medium height, and handsome. He bore a striking resemblance to his mother, Mrs. Maylie.

"Mother, how good to see you!" he exclaimed when he entered the house. "But, of course, I have also come to see Rose. She must hear me out!"

The next evening Oliver was studying. An odd feeling overcame him, and he looked out the window. There, staring right at him with the madman who had cursed him at the inn, was Fagin!

"Help! Oh, help!" cried Oliver, who knew that Fagin had recognized him immediately. Harry came running, but the pair were gone. Oliver now feared that his happy life was about to end.

FS-17020 Oliver Twist (retold)

"Don't worry," said Harry confidently, "they cannot touch you here."

The next day, Harry spoke with Rose and asked her to marry him, but her answer was no, as he feared it might be.

"Harry, I cannot marry you. You are so above me in station, I would keep you behind in your career. If I were not who I am, it would be different. I am a friendless girl with nothing and no family. My lack of a suitable family would disgrace you."

Harry was devastated. He had loved Rose for a long time.

"I must leave now, Rose," he said, "but I won't give up. Promise me you'll think about my proposal and perhaps reconsider in a year or less!"

Rose promised, but she knew in her heart that it was hopeless.

Harry approached Oliver and said, "I will be gone for a while. Write to me at general delivery every two weeks or so and let me know how things are going here. I must know that my mother and Rose are well. But I trust you, Oliver, to tell no one of my whereabouts."

Oliver promised to do as Harry asked and assured him that he could be trusted.

As Harry left, he glanced back at Rose's window. She watched him, weeping.

FS-17020 Oliver Twist (retold)

Name _____

1. Rose refused to marry Harry because she thought she wasn't good enough for him. What do you think of her attitude? Do you think this happens today? If so, give an example of how it might happen. _____

    _____

    _____

    _____

2. There seem to be many secrets in this story. Write about the people so far who have secrets and what they might be.

    Fagin _____

    _____

    Old Sally _____

    _____

    Oliver _____

    _____

    Rose _____

    _____

    Harry _____

    _____

FS-17020 Oliver Twist (retold)

CHAPTER 18

OLD SALLY'S SECRET

Mr. Bumble was disappointed in his new life. He had married Mrs. Corney and was now the master of the workhouse.

"I sold myself cheap," he said aloud, "for six teaspoons, a pair of sugar tongs and a milk pot, a bit of furniture, and twenty pounds. Dirt cheap!"

The sweet Mrs. Bumble shrieked like a fishwife, "Cheap! You would have been expensive at any price!"

Mr. Bumble gave her his most frightening scowl. Without warning, Mrs. Bumble burst into tears. Mr. Bumble was not moved, but rather told her, "Cry away, if you must." She then beat him soundly and told him to get out, which he did, gladly.

Mr. Bumble walked to the workhouse. Seeing some women talking, he ordered them to stop. He then saw, directly in front of him, Mrs. Bumble.

"What do you want?" she roared. "Don't interfere with me! Get out!"

Mr. Bumble took refuge at the tavern. There, he was approached by a man in a cloak.

"You there!" the man commanded. "I need information about a boy who was born here about ten years ago." Mr. Bumble said he knew someone who'd spoken to the nurse who'd attended the boy's birth, but the nurse was dead.

Mr. Bumble discovered that the man's name was Monks. And he would pay well for useful information about Sally's death.

The very next night, Mr. and Mrs. Bumble met Monks by the river.

"I was alone with her when she died," whispered Mrs. Bumble. "She mumbled something about gold, then died. I saw that she was clutching something in her hand. It was a piece of paper, a ticket from a pawnbroker's shop. I took the ticket and got it back." With that, she produced a small bag. Monks eagerly opened it.

"It's a gold locket," he said. "Two locks of hair and a gold wedding ring are in it. The ring says 'Agnes.' Good. You've done well."

"Will I get into trouble for giving it to you?" asked Mrs. Bumble.

The answer was no. Monks threw the treasure into the water and ordered the couple to tell no one what had happened and to leave quickly. The Bumbles gladly did as they were told.

Name _____

1. What kind of person did the new Mrs. Bumble turn out to be?

   _____

   _____

2. Why do you think that Mr. Bumble was so strong with the poor people and so weak with his wife? _____

   _____

3. Why was Mrs. Bumble eager to part with the locket and its contents? How did she feel about Monks? _____

   _____

4. How has Mr. Bumble's life become worse than it was before his marriage? _____

   _____

   _____

5. Why do you think Monks wanted the locket, only to throw it away? _____

   _____

6. Do you think the Bumbles will keep the secret? Why? _____

   _____

7. Mr. Bumble probably had a lot he'd like to tell Mrs. Bumble. Write a note from him to her detailing his complaints about their marriage. Use the back of this page if necessary.

   _____

   _____

FS-17020 Oliver Twist (retold)

CHAPTER 19

ROSE AND NANCY

Bill Sikes, being in a bad mood, decided to take it out on Nancy. Fortunately, Fagin and his boys came to visit and brought food and drink.

"I've been sick and need money," Sikes said to Fagin. "Nancy will get it for me, as she's the only one I trust." Nancy followed Fagin home to get the money and heard a familiar voice while there. It was Monks.

"I'm expecting a visitor," Fagin said, hoping Nancy would leave. When she didn't, he and Monks went to another part of the house.

Nancy threw her shawl and hat under the table. She went upstairs but was back again before Fagin returned. And then she was off.

Back home, Nancy nervously tended to the sick Sikes. After he fell asleep, she stopped at a hotel and asked where she could find Rose Maylie.

After some difficulty, she met Rose and confessed that it was she who waylaid Oliver when he was supposed to return to Mr. Brownlow's and returned him to Fagin.

"I'm sorry for all I did," said Nancy, "and I want to make it right. I always liked the boy and stood up for him. I heard about a plan they're hatching from a man named Monks. He knows you. That's how I knew how to find you. He knows who Oliver really is, too."

"Stay here, Nancy, it's dangerous for you to go back," said Rose, but Nancy knew she must return to Sikes or he would be suspicious.

"In case you need me," said Nancy, "I'll walk on London Bridge every night at eleven o'clock." Nancy then left.

Giles entered and, much to Rose's surprise, said that Mr. Brownlow had returned to his home. Rose promptly went to see him.

"How happy I am that the boy is well," Mr. Brownlow responded. "But we must get the villains and bring them to justice. Then Oliver will be free of them." Rose arranged a meeting with Harry, Mr. Grimwig, Mr. Brownlow, and Dr. Losberne. They put their plan into action.

 FS-17020 Oliver Twist (retold)

Name _____

Rose and Nancy were two women who were very important in Oliver's life. Answer the questions about them below.

1. Why was Nancy important? _____
   _____

2. Why was Rose important? _____
   _____

3. What did the two women have in common? _____
   _____

4. Which woman had more to lose by helping Oliver? Why? _____
   _____
   _____

5. Who do you like better, Rose or Nancy? Why? _____
   _____
   _____

6. Why did Nancy always return to Bill although she knew she'd be beaten by him?
   _____
   _____

FS-17020 Oliver Twist (retold)

CHAPTER 20

NOAH JOINS THE GANG

Noah Claypole trudged through the streets of London with Charlotte lagging behind him as he carried the bulk of their belongings. Charlotte had robbed Mr. Sowerberry, and the couple needed to be on the move. They stopped at The Three Cripples tavern, frequented by Fagin. Noah was hoping to find dishonest work and told Charlotte that he'd like to be the leader of a gang. Fagin, who had been listening, approached him.

"You look like a clever lad," suggested Fagin. Noah assured him that he was. Fagin liked the way Noah controlled Charlotte and sensed that the ugly boy could be useful.

"If you work for me," he told the greedy Noah, "you can keep half of all you make, and so can the lady."

"I would like to do light things, something in the sneaking way, not too dangerous or too hard, mind you," Noah stated.

"I can use you. My best lad, the Dodger, was caught at his trade and there will be a hearing tomorrow. I expect he'll be hanged. Go to the court and find out his fate."

The next day the Dodger made a mockery of the hearing.

"I'm an Englishman, I got rights!" he protested, and was ordered to be still. "Go ahead, put me in jail. I wouldn't go free even if you begged me!" He was led off to jail. Noah returned to Fagin and reported the goings-on. The Dodger had, with his insolence, established himself as a hero in the eyes of his peers.

But Noah's next assignment was much more dastardly. Bill Sikes had noticed that Nancy was acting weird. One night, when she attempted to go out, he kept her forcibly until after midnight. But the next night she did sneak out and met Rose Maylie and Mr. Brownlow. Noah had been ordered to follow her and listen.

"I can't stay long," she whispered, "but I have information. If you want to get the secret from Monks, he can be watched at The Three Cripples." Nancy described Monks.

"Nancy," said Mr. Brownlow, "we can get you out of this life to safety. We'll send you to another country if necessary."

Nancy laughed. "It's too late for me. Just give me something, Miss Rose, to remember you by. I want no money. Be sure Monks doesn't know it was I who pointed him out."

Rose gave Nancy her handkerchief and said good-bye. Nancy left. So did Noah, having heard everything. He raced back to Fagin.

Name _____

1. What actions on the part of Noah have shown, thus far, that he is a coward? _____

   _____

   _____

2. Do you think Noah has a conscience? Explain. _____

   _____

   _____

3. Were you surprised that Charlotte, rather than Noah, robbed Mr. Sowerberry? Explain. _____

   _____

   _____

4. Nancy is an interesting character in the story. She led a terrible life and her friends were all criminals, yet she had a soft spot for Oliver and liked Rose Maylie (a woman very different from herself). Write about what you think Nancy's character was like and what made her what she was.

   Was she capable of changing her life? _____

   _____

   _____

   _____

   _____

   _____

   _____

FS-17020 Oliver Twist (retold)

CHAPTER 21

NANCY'S FATE

Fagin was furious when he heard Noah's report about Nancy's treachery. Later, he asked Sikes, "What would you do if one of us betrayed you?" Sikes answered that he would beat their brains out and go to jail for sure. Fagin hinted that it was Nancy who gave them up. Noah was woken up to repeat every last detail of what he had seen and heard the night before. Sikes charged home in a rage.

When Sikes arrived, Nancy was still asleep. She awoke and was happy to see that Bill was home. Her happiness was short-lived, as she realized that something was wrong.

"You were watched tonight," he revealed, "and every word you said was heard." Bill advanced toward Nancy with murder in his heart. "Please, Bill—Miss Maylie said we could leave this place. We could start a new life, Bill, you and me. Spare me, Bill!" Nancy cried.

But Sikes was enraged. He hit Nancy twice with his pistol. She wiped at the blood on her face with Rose's handkerchief. There was no stopping him. He struck her again and again with a club until she was dead. He had killed the only person in the world who cared about him. He then fled to the countryside with his dog. If he could get money from Fagin, he could flee to France. He then decided that he could be identified by the presence of the dog. He decided to tie a rock around the dog and drown him. But the dog sensed danger and ran away. Sikes went on by himself.

FS-17020 Oliver Twist (retold)

Name _____

1. How could Nancy have avoided being killed by Bill? _____

_____

_____

_____

_____

2. What do you think will happen to Bill? What do you think should happen to him? Do you think he'll be sorry for killing Nancy?

_____

_____

_____

_____

_____

_____

3. Why did Bill think he'd be safe in France?

_____

_____

_____

_____

4. In most stories, the main character appears throughout the story. In *Oliver Twist*, there are entire chapters where Oliver is nowhere to be seen. Why do you think Dickens did this? What do you think of telling a story this way? _____

_____

_____

_____

_____

_____

_____

_____

CHAPTER 22

TRUTHS AND JUSTICE

Mr. Brownlow returned home with Monks in tow. He had told Monks that he had two choices: He could cooperate with him or be turned over to the law on charges of fraud and robbery. They entered the room and Mr. Brownlow locked the door. Monks complained, "This is shabby treatment from my father's oldest friend." Slowly, the story unfolded: When Monks' father was a boy, his sister, who was engaged to Mr. Brownlow, died. Mr. Brownlow sentimentally remained friends with the dead girl's brother until he, too, died.

"Your name is Edward Leeford, not Monks," Mr. Brownlow recalled. "My friend was married to a woman he didn't even like. You were their only child. They ultimately separated. Your father then met and married a lovely girl who had a younger sister. Your father inherited some money but died before he could claim it. Your mother arrived just before he died. All the property went to your mother and you. Your father left with me a portrait of the girl he loved. I attempted to see her, but the family had vanished. Years later, I witnessed the resemblance between that portrait and young Oliver—your father's rightful heir."

"You cannot prove any of this," said Monks defiantly. "Just because Oliver resembles the girl in the portrait . . ."

"Oliver is your brother! You must make restitution to him." said Mr. Brownlow. "He was the son of your father and the unfortunate woman he loved. There was a will! Your mother destroyed it so you and she would inherit everything!" With this, Mr. Brownlow stared at Monks.

Just then, Dr. Losberne entered.

"Good news! Sikes's dog has been spotted, and Sikes cannot be far behind! The arrest of Fagin is certain as well!" Monks almost collapsed at the news. He agreed to cooperate.

Meanwhile, all was lost for the gang. Fagin had been arrested, as was Noah Claypole. Chitling and Bates escaped. Betsy went to see Nancy and, finding her dead, went mad and had to be taken away in a straitjacket. Fagin was most certain to be hanged.

Bill Sikes had eluded the police. His dog showed up and then Sikes himself. Charley Bates attacked him for killing Nancy.

"You monster! I'll turn you in!" screamed Bates. Suddenly, the police began banging at the door. "Break it down!" yelled Bates. "He's in here!" Sikes threw the boy into a vacant room and locked the door. Then he tied a rope around himself to lower his body to the ground. But his luck had run out. The murderer lost his footing and plunged to the ground, the rope, like a noose around his neck, hanged him.

FS-17020 Oliver Twist (retold)

The matter of Oliver was settled in court. Mr. Brownlow told Oliver about who he really was and that his mother was a woman from a good family. Monks agreed that this was the truth. The magistrate decided that although Oliver was entitled to all the money his father left, Monks should not be left penniless.

And what of the criminals? Monks left the country. He couldn't give up his wicked ways. His mother had taught him to hate the brother he never knew. He soon lost all his money and went back to the criminal life. He died in prison. Fagin was hanged and no one was sorry. Noah Claypole was pardoned for testifying against Fagin. He became a police informer. The Bumbles lost their positions and became inmates of the workhouse where they once tortured others. Charley Bates gave up his life of crime and became a herdsman in the country.

Oliver's hard life was now behind him forever. The only thing that marred his happiness was the news that his little friend, Dick, was dead. However, Oliver was adopted by Mr. Brownlow and they moved out to the country to be near the Maylies' home. There was one more secret to tell: Rose was the younger sister of Oliver's mother, Agnes, and now she also knew she came from a good family. She gladly accepted her new role as Oliver's aunt. She was now free to marry Harry Maylie and did so in good time.

And now, inside an old country church, there is an empty tomb. On the marble stone above it is written, "Agnes."

Name _____

1. Write a summary of the story. _____

_____

_____

_____

_____

_____

_____

_____

_____

_____

_____

_____

_____

2. What would you change in the story?

_____

_____

3. Would you like to read more stories by Charles Dickens? Explain your answer. _____

_____

_____

_____

_____

_____

_____

_____

FS-17020 Oliver Twist (retold)

Oliver Twist Today

Have students write a modern-day story of *Oliver Twist*, telling about a boy or girl with the problems of today's kids. Ask students to analyze *Oliver Twist* and write their stories using the same general "formula."

Character Analysis

Ask students to write the names of at least seven characters from the story. Have students describe the characters and their roles in the story.

Read All About It!

The story of Oliver's discovery of his family, including half-brother Monks, and what becomes of Sikes, Nancy, and Fagin are big news! Have students write newspaper articles about what happened to each character. Remind them to write headlines and to include the "five W's"—Who, What, When, Where, Why—in their stories. Ask them to write the articles in columns, newspaper style. Provide newspaper stories as models. Have students write and format their newspaper articles on a computer.

Oliver Twist—The Play

This story is a perfect vehicle for a stage play. Discuss the play with students and organize them into groups responsible for writing the play, acting in it, making props and scenery, and handling publicity. After the script is written and you've approved it, have tryouts and put your play into production. Arrange for your students to perform the play for other students, for administrators, or for parents to ensure an audience for their efforts.

Picture Books

Share the classics with younger students. Ask for volunteers among your students to make illustrations and write a simple version of this story for a picture book to share with lower-grade students. The team must work together so the book will have a consistent look. This is perfect for collaborative work and may involve many students. Students who are not involved in the writing and illustrating may wish to visit other classes and read the book aloud.

The Many Lives of *Oliver Twist*

There have been several versions of *Oliver Twist* on film, and they are available on video as dramas, musicals, and even cartoons. Show one or more of these videos in your class and ask students to compare them with the story written by Charles Dickens. Have students write reviews of the videos.

FS-17020 Oliver Twist (retold)